Anonymous

The Armenian Liturgy

Translated into English

Anonymous

The Armenian Liturgy
Translated into English

ISBN/EAN: 9783337292645

Printed in Europe, USA, Canada, Australia, Japan

Cover: Foto ©Lupo / pixelio.de

More available books at **www.hansebooks.com**

THE

ARMENIAN LITURGY

TRANSLATED

INTO ENGLISH

VENICE

PRINTED

AT THE ARMENIAN MONASTERY OF St LAZARUS

OF THE ANTIQUITY

AND OF THE PRECIOUS CHARACTERISTICS

OF THE

ARMENIAN LITURGY.

The Armenian Liturgy may be ranged among the most ancient, and the most beautiful of all the Liturgies of the Oriental Churches.

Father Lebrun, a celebrated Benedictine, has proved its venerable antiquity, and he says that it was written towards the end of the fourth, or the beginning of the fifth century. But when we derive from original sources a more precise knowledge of this antiquity, we find that the rites of the Armenian Mass, formed on the model of the liturgies of S^t. Basil and of S^t. Athanasius, already existed at the commencement of the fourth century, in the time of S^t. Gregory the Illuminator, the apostle of Armenia, or, at least, in the time of S^t. Nerses the Great, who lived before S^t. Chrysostom. Later, that

1*

is to say, at the beginning of the fifth century, the Armenian Liturgy was better arranged, and augmented by many things borrowed from the Liturgy of S^t. Chrysostom, which proves the perfect accordance of these two liturgies, especially as regards the first part of the Mass, called the Mass of the Catechumens.

The authors of this reform were the same Armenian doctors who, about this time, translated the Holy Scriptures into the Armenian language, with that elegance of style which is also so apparent in the Liturgy; for this century was the classic epoch of Armenian literature.

Such, then, are the two principal characteristics of the Armenian Liturgy: venerable antiquity in all its rites, ceremonies and prayers, and a beauty of language quite classic, worthy of the purity of the Golden Age in which it was written.

The Armenians have always preserved, in all its integrity, the majestic elegance of the rites and ceremonies of the ancient Church, without changing the usages of the first ages of Christianity.

Foreigners of all nations who assist at the High Mass of the Armenian rite, testify their admiration of it, and the impression made on their minds by the mysterious ceremonies, and by the simple majesty of the oriental ritual. Besides the elegance of style in which this liturgy is written, all the prayers, from that beginning: « Lord God of Hosts » to the

Communion, show an elevation of ideas quite original, and great sublimity of sentiment. The hymns very nearly approach to the poetry of the Bible, and the prayers of the celebrant and of all the clergy, participate in the grandeur of the mysteries of the Sacrifice.

To confirm the authority of what we advance, we appeal to the testimony of the same French liturgist already cited, in the 10 dissertation of his work (1).

(1) The Armenian translation of the Bible has been cited with admiration by the most celebrated commentators, and particularly by the learned Hottinger, Galia, Piques a Doctor of the Sorbonne, Lacroze, etc. The celebrated Benedictine liturgist said, that the Armenian translation might be made use of to correct the faults which have crept into the original greek, of the version of the septuagint.

GENERAL VIEW

OF THE RELIGIOUS CEREMONIES

OF THE ARMENIAN CHURCH

DURING

HIGH MASS.

Before we examine, in detail, the ceremonies practised by the Armenians during High Mass, we think it well to give a true idea of the musical instruments which they use, of the oriental songs and hymns, of the vestments of the clergy, etc.

The form of the Armenian Churches, nearly approaches that of the Greek. There is but one altar in the midst of the choir, to which they ascend by steps.

This altar is sometimes hidden during the Mass by two curtains: a large one, drawn all across the choir, separating the Sanctuary, the Celebrant, and the Deacons from the rest of the clergy and the people: and a small one which surrounds the altar, and separates the Celebrant from the Deacons who assist him in the ceremony. Each curtain opens on two sides as will be presently seen during the celebration of the ritual.

The Cross, the silver candlesticks, and the images of the saints form the decoration of the altar. The Chalice, the Cross and the Gospel during the Mass, are always covered with a light veil embroidered in gold; they are objects of the highest respect, and can only be touched with this veil. At the right side of the altar is a smaller one, in the form of a niche, where are placed the offerings of bread and wine destined to be consecrated, and which have been presented by one of the principal people: they remain there till the Deacons come to carry them to the great altar.

The episcopal throne, covered with an embroidered canopy, is also on this side.

The rest of the Church is divided into two parts, one for the men, the other for the women.

The Armenian songs are composed in a musical style conformable to the genius and taste of the Orientals, which is perhaps more natural, but which does not, in general, please European ears: these chants are mostly accompanied by metallic instruments called *Kechotz, Zinzgha,* etc.: the first is the instrument called in latin *Flabellum,* used also in the Greek Church: it is a Cherubim with many wings loaded with small bells, and is fastened to the end of a long stick, which they agitate at different parts of the Mass, in the same way as the latin bells, of which they hold the place. The second instrument is composed of two plates of bronze, like the cymbals in military bands, which struck one against the other, give an inspiriting sound: there are other harmonious and wind instruments, but the organ is not used.

The form of the sacerdotal vestments is very majestic. The clergy and under-deacon, wear albs, of stuff more or less precious, which fall to the heels. These albs have the cross embroidered on the back and on the chest, as well as on the shoulders. The deacons, besides their alb which is generally richer, wear also the long stole, embroidered with crosses, which they put on obliquely, making it pass from the left shoulder under the right arm. If the Celebrant is a Bishop the two first Deacons also wear the sacerdotal bonnet on the head.

All colours, excepting black, are used in the religious ceremonies, and there is no distinction of colours for the festivals. The number of deacons is not fixed: there are generally six, but there may be more or less, according to the festival, and the rank of the Celebrant. The Deacons, after having put on their robes, assist the Celebrant to put on his.

The sacerdotal bonnet is round, and richly embroidered with gold, and pearls; at the top there is a figure of the world, made of enamel, of gold, or of diamonds, and surmounted by a small cross. The Bishops wear the latin mitre. The alb of the Celebrant is generally of linen or of different stuffs, the sleeves are of the same stuff as the cope. The stole, embroidered with crosses, is put round the neck and falls down before, to the feet: this stole, as well as the alb, is fastened by the golden buckle of the belt. The Bishops also wear, on the right side, an ornament attached to the belt, something in the shape of a shield called *Gonkèr*. After these vestments, the Celebrant puts on the *super-humeral,* a large collar of precious stuff which rests on the shoulders, then he takes the long and flowing cope which envelopes his whole person and which is not closed before, like that of the Greeks. The Priest, whilst putting on these different objects, recites prayers adapted to the mystical signification of each ornament.

The Bishops also wear the long mantle or *pallium,* which hangs down before and behind, passing across the shoulders. The crosier of the Bishops is like that of the Latins. The Doctors or *Vartabieds* have a particular sort of crosier formed of two serpents intertwined, at the end of a long stick, the serpent being the emblem of prudence, a virtue indispensable to those who preach the word of God. These emblematic signs, as well as the Cross and the emblem of the diocese ([1]), precede the Celebrant

(1) Every Archbishop has a particular Emblem of his diocese, and the doctoral crosier. ʿʿhese prelates are always preceded by four distinc-

when he goes to the altar, and when he descends to incense the people. The young clerks who carry them, together with those who carry the mantle and the mitre, are ranged on the steps of the altar during the Mass.

When the Celebrant, accompanied by the inferior ministers, ascends the steps of the altar, after the Introït, they for the first time, close the great curtain, to prepare for the offerings: when it is again opened, you see the Celebrant holding the censor, to incense the altar: if the Celebrant is a Bishop, they close the great curtain a second time, to take away his episcopal distinctions, so that, at the reopening of the curtain, he appears as a simple priest.

After the benediction which the Celebrant gives the people with the Holy Sacrament, they draw the little curtain to leave the Celebrant alone at the moment of his communion, after which the curtain is withdrawn and the Priest shows himself, turned towards the people, with the remains of the Sacred Host in his hands, and, if there are any communicants, they receive the Divine Sacrament. But there are be no communicants, the Celebrant blesses the people a second time with the Holy Sacrament, and the great curtain is drawn.

After the ablutions, the Celebrant covers his head with the bonnet, if he be a Bishop, he resumes his

tive signs: the Archiepiscopal crosier, the Doctoral crosier, the Cross and the Emblem of their diocese.

2

mitre and episcopal distinctions; then he turns towards the people, holding the Holy Gospel, when they open the great curtain to end the Mass.

On Christmas-Eve, and Easter-Eve, tho Mass, which the Armenians celebrate in the evening, begins with the curtain drawn, and outside they read the prophecies of Daniel and others, according to the mystery of the day. At the moment the feast is announced, after the Introït the curtain is withdrawn and the altar appears illuminated.

During Lent, the altar remains hidden by the great curtain as a figure of the expulsion of our first parents from Paradise, and all the Sundays in Lent, except Palm-sunday, the Mass is celebrated with the curtain drawn.

THE ORDER AND CEREMONY

OF PREPARATION FOR THE

HOLY SACRIFICE OF THE ALTAR.

～～≻ᢢᢞ≺～～

At the celebration of the Holy Sacrifice the Priest thus robes himself without pomp or ceremonial: he enters with his Assistant Ministers into the Sacristy where the vestments and ornaments are kept; and after each has robed himself according to his order, having preluded with the Antiphon: Sacerdotes tui induantur justitiam, *etc. they recite alternately the* CXXXI' Psalm : Memento, Domine, David, *etc. with the* Gloria Patri, *etc.*

Then the Deacon says:

Let us unite to ask with faith that God may bestow upon us His merciful grace, that the all-powerful God may save us and show us His mercy. O

Lord, have mercy upon us according to the greatness of Thy mercy; and let us say all together:

Lord, have mercy upon us!

This invocation is repeated twelve times. Then the Priest says the following prayer:

Jesus Christ our Lord, who, clothed with light as with a bright garment, hath appeared on earth in profound humility, and hath deigned to hold converse with man; who hath made Thyself Sovereign and Eternal High Priest after the order of Melchisedek, and hath bestowed gifts on Thy holy Church; O Lord all-powerful! who hath permitted us to robe ourselves in the same celestial garb, make me, thy useless servant, worthy of the spiritual ministry of Thy glory: now that I dare prepare myself, may I be free from iniquity which is the robe of abomination, and may I be mantled in Thy light! Take from me my stains, blot out my sins, that I may be worthy of the light that Thou hath prepared; grant me to enter with the sacerdotal robes into the ministry of Thy sanctuary in company with those who, always less spot, have observed Thy commandments; may I be found ready to penetrate into the celestial nuptial-chamber with the wise virgins to glorify Thee, Jesus, my Lord, who hath borne and effaced the sins of all, I implore Thee, for Thou art the sanctifier of our souls,

and to Thee our beneficent God belong glory, power
and honour, now and for ever throughout all ages.
So be it.

The Deacons then invest the Priest with his ornaments, reciting the
appropriate Psalms. They first put upon his head the sacerdotal crown
and the Priest says:

Lord! put upon my head the helmet of salvation to combat the forces of the enemy, through the
grace of our Lord Jesus Christ, to whom glory, power and honour are due now and for ewer, throughout
all ages. So be it.

Then they present him with the Alb, and the Priest says:

Clothe me, O Lord, with the robe of salvation
and with the tunic of gladness, and bind me with
the robe of redemption, through the grace of our
Lord Jesus Christ, etc.

Then the Maniple, and he says:

Lord! strengthen my hands and wash me from
all stain, so that I may serve Thee in perfect purity
of soul and body, through the grace, etc.

Then the Stole, and he says:

Lord, ornament my neck with justice, and purify my heart from all stain of sin, through the grace, etc.

Then the Girdle, and he says:

May the girdle of faith gird my heart and mind, and prevent impure thoughts, and may the virtue of Thy grace ever dwell there, through the grace, etc.

Then the Cope, and he says:

O Lord! through Thy mercy cover me with a robe of splendour, and fortify me against the assaults of the evil spirit, that I may be worthy to glorify Thy glorious name, through the grace, etc.

My soul shall rejoice in the Lord, for He has invested me with the vesture of salvation, and the robe of gladness, He has decked my head with a crown, as a bridegroom, and as a bride He has ornamented me, through the grace, etc.

While the Celebrant robes himself, the Clerks sing in the Choir, the following hymn.

O profound and incomprehensible mystery, without beginning! Above us Thou hath illuminated the Principalities in the nuptial chamber with inaccessible light, and Thou hath surrounded the choirs of Angels with incomparable glory.

By Thine ineffable and marvellous power Thou hath created Adam in the likeness of Thy sovereignty, and Thou hath robed him with pomp and glory in Eden, dwelling of delights.

By the Passion of the Holy One, Thine only Son, all creatures have been renewed, and man is become again immortal, and has been clothed with a vesture of which he can never be despoiled.

O Holy Spirit, God! who under the form of tongues of fire of ineffable fecundity, Thou hath descended on the Apostles in the holy guest-chamber, pour forth Thy wisdom also upon us, while we robe ourselves with this tunic.

Holiness becomes Thy dwelling, and since Thou alone art enveloped in splendour, and surrounded with glorious holiness, gird us with truth.

Thou who hath stretched out Thy creating arms to the stars, strengthen our arms so that in upraising our hands we may become intercessors before Thee.

May the diadem which encircles our head, protect our thoughts, and may the stole, symbol of the Cross guard our senses; stole like to that of Aaron, beautiful, and brilliant with golden flowers to adorn the Sanctuary.

O sole God, true and sovereign master of all creatures, who hath invested us with the cope, symbol of love, to make us worthy ministers of Thy holy mystery!

Preserve, Heavenly King! Thy Church immovable and give peace to the worshippers of Thy name.

All being robed with the sacred vestments, go to the Altar. The Priest, washing his hands, recites, in a low voice, alternately with the Deacon, the XXVth Psalm.

Anthem: Lavabo in innocentia manus meas, *etc.*

DEACON. — Judica me Deus, *etc.*; Gloria Patri.

Then the Mass commences.

The Priest, extending his arms:

Accept O Lord! our prayers and save us through the intercession of the Holy Mother of God.

DEACON. — May the Holy Mother of God and all the saints be our intercessors with the Heavenly Father, that He may deign to be merciful to us, and in pity save His Creatures. Lord God all-powerful! save us and have mercy upon us!

PRIEST. — Receive, Lord, our prayers, through the intercession of the Holy Mother of God, the Immaculate Mother of Thine only Son, and through the prayers of all the saints, hear us, Lord, and have mercy on us: pardon us, be favourable to us, and blot out our sins, and make us worthy to glorify Thee in the thanksgiving which we offer Thee together

with Thy Son and the Holy Ghost, now and for
ever.

The Officiating Priest, again joining his hands, and turning towards
the assistant Clergy, inclining himself, begins the Confession.

I Confess in the presence of God and of the holy
Mother of God, before all the saints, and before you
Fathers and Brethren, all the sins I have committed;
for I have sinned in thought, in word and in deed,
and in whatever way men generally sin: I have
sinned, I have sinned, and I pray you to ask pardon
of God for me.

The eldest Priest in the Choir approaches and gives the absolution
demanded by the Officiating Priest.

May all-powerful God have mercy on you, and
grant you the pardon of all your sins, past and present, and preserve you from them in future: may He
confirm you in every good work, and lead you to the
repose of a future life. So be it.

The Officiating Priest, raising the crucifix in his right hand; gives
his benediction saying.

May the God of love free you, and purify you
from all your sins: may He give you time to do penance and to do good works: may the all-powerful
and all-merciful God guide your future life by the

grace of His Holy Spirit. To him be glory throughout all ages. So be it.

The elder Priest adds:

Remember us in the presence of the immortal Lamb of God.

The Priest still turned towards the assistant Clergy answers:

May your remembrance be present before the immortal Lamb of God!

The Clerks recite the CXIXth Psalm: Jubilate Deo, etc.

DEACON. — In the name of this holy Church let us pray God that He may deliver us from sin and save us by His merciful grace. All-powerful Lord, our God, save us and have mercy on us.

The Priest, extending his arms:

Within the precincts of this temple, and in presence of these sacred and divine emblems, bowing in the holy place, we adore with trembling, and we glorify Thy holy, admirable and victorious resurrection, and we offer Thee benediction and glory, together with the Father and the Holy Spirit now and in endless ages.

The Priest says the XLIId Psalm, with the Anthem: *Introibo*, etc.
The Deacon says the Psalm: *Judica me Deus*, etc.
At every two verses they ascend a step of the altar.

At the top of the steps, the Deacon says:

Let us bless the Father of our Lord Jesus Christ, who has made us worthy to present ourselves in the place of praise, and to sing spiritual songs. All-powerful Lord, our God, save us and have mercy on us.

The Priest with extended arms, advances nearer to the altar, and says the following prayer aloud:

In the Tabernaclé of holiness, and in the place of praise, the habitation of Angels, the Sanctuary of expiation and of propitiation for man, before these sacred and divine emblems prostrated at the foot of the holy altar, we adore with trembling, and glorify Thy holy, admirable and victorious resurrection; and we offer Thee benediction and glory, together with the Father and the Holy Spirit now and in endless ages.

This prayer ended, if the Celebrant is a Priest, they draw the curtain.

If the Celebrant is a Bishop, he kneels before the altar with his four Deacons, and, the two others coming to raise the mitre, he takes the holy Apron and spreads it on his knees; he also spreads the holy Pallium on his breast. Then approaching with the assistants the altar of oblation, he washes his hands. Finally, at the foot of the altar, he says in a low voice, the following prayer addressed to the Holy Spirit, the Perfecter of the holy mysteries.

The two following prayers were composed by the celebrated Doctor St. Gregory Nareghatzi, who flourished in the Xth century.

O Lord all-powerful, beneficent and full of love: sovereign of the universe, Creator of all things visible and invisible, Redeemer and Preserver, Protector and Pacificator, Powerful Spirit of the Father! assembled here in Thy redoutable presence, we implore Thee with out-stretched arms and deep groans. Full of fear and awe we approach Thee, to offer the Sacrifice due to Thine Omnipotence as equal on the throne of glory and in works to the immutable and glorious grandeur of the Father; for Thou art the interpreter of the profound mysteries of the will of the all-powerful Father of Emmanuel, who sent Thee, being Himself the Redeemer, Vivifier and Operator of all things. By Thee has been revealed the triple personality of the consubstantial Divinity, triple personality, in which Thou art one and incomprehensible. In Thee and by Thee the first generation of the Patriarchal line, endued with the spirit of prophecy, clearly announced things past and future. Spirit of God! Thou wert predicted by Moses; Spirit that movedst upon the waters, boundless virtue, who by Thy mysterious shadow, vivifying afar all around, and under Thy wings, affectionately protecting new generations, hath revealed the mystery of regenerating baptism. As a figure of this mystery, before Thou spreadedst out the curtain of the firmament, Thy sovereign will created out of nothing, all living being. By Thy virtue all mankind drawn out of chaos, will be renewed in the miraculous act of the resurrection, at the same moment which marketh the last day of their terrestrial and mortal life, and the first of the life celestial and immortal. To Thee, as to His Father, the first-born Son, coexistant and consubstantial with the Father, has obeyed, under a human form, and in unity of will. He proclaimed Thee true God, equal and consubstantial with His Father, all-powerful; and declared unworthy of pardon all blasphemy against Thee, thus shutting the sacrilegious mouths of Thy depreciators, by Him declared enemies of God; whilst all blasphemy, proffered by the impious against Himself, has been pardoned by Him, the Just, the Immaculate, the Good Shepherd, Reclaimer of all wandering souls, who was delivered for our offences, and was raised again for our justification. To Him be glory through Thee, and to Thee benediction, with the all-powerful Father, throughout all ages. So be it.

They then say this prayer on the same subject that by a livelier confidence it may sink deeply into the heart, and excite the desire of announcing and obtaining a twofold peace.

We pray and implore with all our soul and with

tears and sighs, Thy glorious creative essence, O
tender, incorruptible, uncreated, eternal Spirit of
mercy, who, with ineffable sighs intercedest for us
with the Father of all grace; Thou that preservest
the saints, purifiest sinners, and makest them the
temples of the living and vivifying will of the supreme
Father. O! deliver us from all works impure and
displeasing in Thy sight, that the illuminating rays
of Thy grace may not be weakened in us by the
infirmity of our weak intelligence, for we know that
Thou unitest Thyself to us only by means of prayer,
and the sweet smelling savour of a pure life. Since
one Person of the Holy Trinity is sacrificed, and
another receives him, taking pleasure in us through
the reconciling blood of His Only Begotten Son; O!
do Thou, also, accept our prayer; cleanse us and make
us a precious and agreeable habitation, by a perfect
preparation, that we may rejoice in the feast of the
Heavenly Lamb and receive without peril of perdi-
tion, this manna of the new redemption, manna
which renders us immortal. May this fire consume
and destroy all trace of human misery, as it did with
the Prophet Isaiah, by the burning coal applied by
the Angel, so that Thy clemency may be manifested,
as by His divine Son is revealed the bounty of the
Father, who has admitted the Prodigal son to the
paternal inheritance and has raised the impure to
the possession of the celestial throne, which is the
happiness of the Just. I also am one of them; re-

ceive me with them, I who have also cost the blood of the divine Jesus, who have need of greater mercy and to be saved by Thy grace. Grant it, that in all things may be universally revealed Thy Divinity, glorified with the Father with equal honour, and praised with equal will and with equal power.

Aloud:

For to Thee belong clemency, power, love, virtue and glory throughout all ages. So be it.

The Deacons give the mitre to the Officiating Bishop, who rises, and the curtain is drawn. The Clerks then sing melodies, or some hymn relating to the mystery of the Day, whilst the Celebrant, behind the curtain, prepares the bread and wine for the Offering.

HYMNS FOR DIVERS FESTIVALS.

For the Annunciation of the Blessed Virgin Mary.

The sound of joyful news is heard, (*repeated*) announced by Gabriel to the All-Holy. I am sent to Thee, O! Immaculate One: (*repeated*) to prepare a chamber for the Lord.

For the Nativity of our Lord.

To-day a new flower springs from the root of

Jesse, and the daughter of David gives birth to the Son of God.

Christ, the king of glory comes to offer Himself to-day, Himself fulfilling the law by His appearance in the Temple after forty days.

The children of the Hebrews sing the song of the Cherubim: the multitude of the Gentiles rejoice with the inhabitants of the skies.

My song resounds with the roaring of the Lion, (*repeated*) who roared upon the Cross.
On the Cross He roared, (*repeated*) and His roaring penetrated threateningly into the deepest abysses.

To-day a new light shines from a new and admirable Sun. To-day a new lily blossoms in the garden newly planted.

For the Ascension.

To-day the first-born and Only Son of the Father soars to Heaven under the form of the sons of Adam. To-day the battalions of the Angelic choirs of Heaven harmoniously modulate songs of praise.

For Pentecost.

Let us sing to the Holy Spirit harmonious hymns of praise. Let us exalt in sublime words the new creation of all things.

For the Transfiguration.

The beauteous rose flames on its stalk through its leaves of a thousand tints. The trembling roses wave by thousands over the leaves.

For the Assumption of the Holy Virgin.

To-day the Angel Gabriel brought the palm and the crown to the triumphant Virgin. To-day he introduced to the Lord of all, her who was the temple of the Most High, and the dwelling of the Holy Spirit.

For the Day of the Holy Cross.

From the beginning of time the Cross appeared in Paradise, planted by the hand of God, as a sign of consolation to Seth, and a gage of hope to Adam, the first father. In this wood to which our Saviour Jesus was nailed, we put all our confidence, and prostrate, and adore the Sacred Sign which has borne our God.

For Archangels' Day.

In your honour, O holy Archangels, and choirs of Angels, we sing in sweetest tones, the praises of jubilation.

For the Feasts of the Holy Apostles.

O Sun of justice proceeding from the Father, who hath filled Thine Apostles with ineffable grace ! The way of heavenly light has been splendidly shown amidst the people of Armenia, by Thaddoeus and Bartholomew.

For the Feasts of the Prophets.

Interpreters of the ineffable secrets of God, O holy Prophets, ye have been from the remotest time the predictors of future events.

For the Feasts of the Pontiffs.

At the solemnity of your feast we triumph with

spiritual joy, O Father and Teacher, holy Pontiff, (N. N.)

The following Canticle may be substituted for any of the foregoing hymns.

O thou, holy and august Priest, chosen of God, like unto Aaron and to the Prophet Moses!

It was Moses who arranged the mysterious vestment which Aaron always wore.

His tunic was woven with four colours: scarlet, azure, amaranth, and purple.

One thread was placed on another, and the thread of the first row was enriched with a carbuncle: the fringe around was of golden thread.

At the sound of his priestly step, the soil rung beneath; and the face of the Tabernacle was clothed with gladness.

To-day Christ makes our Celebrant appear under the same form.

Thou then, in raising thyself to the Sanctuary, remember our departed ones; in the oblation of the Sacrifice, remember me a sinner, that Christ may be merciful to me and to us at His second coming.

Glory be to the Father, honour to the Son and to the Holy Ghost, now and throughout all ages. May Jesus Christ be blessed of all.

Whilst the Clerks sing, the Celebrant, behind the curtain, prepares himself for the offering, and the Host being brought to him by the chief Deacon, he places it on the Patine, saying:

Commemoration of our Lord Jesus Christ.

Then having taken the wine, he pours some, in the form of a Cross, into the Chalice, adding a little water, and says:

In memory of the Salutary Incarnation of the Lord our God and Redeemer Jesus Christ.

He then recites, in a low voice, the following prayer of St. Chrysostom.

O Lord our God, who hath sent the heavenly bread, our Lord Jesus Christ, the spiritual food of all the universe, as Redeemer, Saviour and Benefactor, to bless and sanctify us; Thyself, Lord, now bless † the oblation here offered, and receive it on Thy heavenly altar; remember in Thy benevolence and Thy love, those who offer it, and those for whom it is offered, and preserve us from sin in the administration of Thy Sacraments; for holy and glorious is the honourable and sovereign grandeur of Thy glory, O Father, Son and Holy Ghost, now and throughout all ages. So be it.

Covering the Chalice with the veil, he recites the XCIId Psalm *Dominus regnavit.*

The curtain is withdrawn.

Incensing the altar, the Celebrant says :

We offer the sweet spiritual perfume of incense
in Thy presence, O Lord Christ, accept it in Thy
holy, celestial and immaterial dwelling as a sweet
odour, and send us, in exchange, the grace and the
gifts of Thy Holy Spirit. To Thee we offer glory,
together with the Father and the Holy Ghost, now,
etc.

The Priest kisses the altar three times, and after having incensed
it, he descends the steps, with the Deacons, to incense the people who
stand and make the sign of the Cross, whilst the Clerks sing the hymn
of incensement.

In the Lord's temple, open to our offerings and
our vows, united as we are to accomplish in obe-
dience and in prayer the mystery of this approaching
and august Sacrifice, let us march together in triumph
round the tribune of thy holy temple with odoriferous incense. Receive with goodness, O Lord, our
prayers, like odoriferous smoke, of sweet myrrh and
cinnamon, and keep us who offer it, so that we may
always serve Thee holily. Through the intercession
of Thy holy and ever-virgin Mother, accept the prayers of Thy ministers.

O Christ our Lord, who by Thy blood hath rendered Thy Church more luminous and more splendid than Heaven, and who from the example of the

celestial choirs, has disposed in it choirs of Apostles, Prophets and holy Teachers; we now united, Priests, Deacons, Clerks and Ecclesiastics, offer incense in Thy presence, O Lord, after the manner of Zacharias of old. May our prayers sound agreeably to Thee, rising with the incense, like the sacrifice of Abel, Noah and Abraham. Through the intercession of Thy heavenly hosts, keep ever in peace the Armenian Church.

Triumph, and glorify thyself with thy sons, O Sion, daughter of light, holy Catholic Mother: deck and adorn thyself, august spouse, splendid tabernacle of light like unto Heaven: because the Anointed God (The Christ) Being of Being, (God of God) sacrifices Himself incessantly without ever being consumed, and to reconcile us to the Father, and for our expiation, He gives His flesh and His precious blood. By virtue of this Sacifice He pardons him, who erected this temple.

The Holy Church acknowledges and confesses the pure Virgin Mary as Mother of God, through whom has been communicated to us the bread of immortality and the cup of consolation. Give blessings to her with spiritual canticle.

After having incensed the people, the Celebrant mounts to the first step of the altar, the Deacons place themselves on both sides of the altar, and the Chief Deacon says aloud:

Give thy benediction, Lord Priest.

And the Priest adds:

Blessed be the reign of the Father, the Son, and the Holy Ghost, now. etc.

Here they say the Introït proper to the feast, which ended, the Deacon says:

Let us again pray the Lord for peace: receive, save us, and have mercy upon us. Give thy benediction, Lord Priest.

PRIEST. — Blessing and glory to the Father, to the Son, and to the Holy Ghost. Peace to all.

CLERKS. — And with thy spirit.

DEACON. — Let us worship God.

CLERKS. — In thy presence, Lord Priest.

The Priest, extending his hands says aloud:

O Lord our God, whose power is boundless and whose glory is incomprehensible, whose mercy is immense, and whose tenderness is infinite; according to Thine ineffable love look upon Thy people and this holy temple, and show towards us and those united with us in prayer, Thy mercy and Thy clemency. For to Thee belong glory, power and honour, now etc.

The Clerks recite the Psalm and Hymn of the day, whilst the Priest, extending his hands, says in a low voice:

O Lord our God, save Thy people and bless Thine inheritance, preserve the fulness of Thy Church and sanctify those who devoutly visit the majesty of Thy house. Glorify us by Thy divine power, and abandon none who hope in Thee; for to The belong power, virtue and glory, now etc.

The Celebrant continues without turning towards the people:

Peace † be to all.

Thou who hath taught us to pray together and in the same spirit, who hath promised us that the prayers of two or three united in Thy name shall be granted, favourably grant the requests of Thy servants, giving us in this world, the knowledge of Thy truth, and in the world to come, life eternal : for Thou art a beneficent God and full of love, and to Thee belong glory, power and honour, now etc.

Then the Priest extending his arms, adds in a low voice :

O Lord our God, who hath ordered in Heaven choirs and battalions of Angels and Archangels for the service of Thy glory, grant that the holy Angels may enter with us, and with us may be the ministers and glorifiers of Thy beneficence.

DEACON. — Give thy benediction, Lord Priest.

PRIEST, ALOUD. — For to Thee belong Power, Virtue and Glory to all Eternity. So be it.

THE DEACON ADDS. — Proschume. — (*Let us be attentive*).

They sing the Trisagion.

THE CLERKS. — Holy Lord, holy and powerful, holy and immortal, have mercy upon us!

Whilst they sing Trisagion, the Deacon who is to read the Gospel, fetches it, accompanied by three others, one of whom incenses it, while the other two wave the Flabellum or instrument of little bells. They go round the altar, and arrived before it, he who holds the censor, invites one of the chief people to come to the same altar and kiss the Gospel, whom the Celebrant blesses.

During this time, the Priest extending his arms, says the following prayer:

Holy Lord, who reigneth in the saints, to whom the Seraphim gives praise in the Song of Trisagion; to whom the Cherubim gives glory, and all the heavenly hosts the tribute of adoration; Thou who hath called all creatures into existence out of chaos, and

3

made man after Thine image and resemblance, and adorned him with Thy grace, by teaching him to seek wisdom and prudence, who didst not abandon him when he became a sinner, but imposedst on him a penance to salvation; who hath rendered us, Thy vile and worthless servants, now worthy to present ourselves before Thy glorious and holy altar and to offer Thee the prescribed praise and adoration; accept, Lord, from the lips of us sinners, this thrice holy benediction, and preserve us by Thy goodness; pardon all our voluntary and involuntary sins: purify us in soul, in spirit and in body; and grant us to serve Thee in holiness all the days of our life, through the intercession of the Holy Mother of God, and of all Thy Saints, in whom, from all Eternity, Thou hath been well-pleased; for Thou art holy, O Lord our God, and to Thee belong glory, power etc.

DEACON. — Let us again pray the Lord for peace.

CLERKS. — Lord, have mercy upon us.

DEACON. — Let us pray the Lord for the peace of the whole world, and the stability of the holy Church.

CLERKS. — Lord, have mercy upon us.

DEACON. — For all saints and orthodox bishops, let us pray the Lord.

CLERKS. — Lord, surround them with Thy mercy.

DEACON. — For our holy Father, Pope N. and for our (Patriarch, Archbishop or Bishop), let us pray the Lord.

CLERKS. — O Lord, protect them and keep them in Thy mercy.

DEACON. — Let us pray God for all Teachers, Priests, Deacons, Clerks and all the faithful.

CLERKS. — O Lord, surround them with Thy mercy.

DEACON. — Let us pray God for pious kings and princes who fear God; for their armies and their chiefs.

CLERKS. — Lord, protect them in Thy mercy.

DEACON. — Let us pray God for the souls of the departed, who, attached to the true faith, sleep in Christ.

CLERKS. — Lord, remember them and have mercy upon them.

DEACON. — Let us pray God for union in our true and holy faith.

CLERKS. — Lord, have mercy upon us.

DEACON. — Let us commend ourselves and one another to the Lord God all-powerful.

CLERKS. — We commend ourselves to Thee O Lord.

DEACON. — Have mercy upon us! O Lord our God, according to Thy great mercy. Let us say with one accord.

CLERKS. — Lord, have mercy upon us.
(This invocation is repeated thrice).

During this time the Priest prays in a law voice, with extended arms :

O Lord our God! accept the prayers which Thy servants address to Thee with uplifted arms, and have mercy upon us according to Thy great mercy. Pour forth Thy clemency upon us and upon this people, steadfast in the expectation of Thine abundant mercy.

DEACON. — Give thy benediction, Lord Priest.

PRIEST. — For Thou art merciful, and lovest man, being God, and to Thee belong glory, power and honour etc.

If the Celebrant be not a Bishop, he remains standing before the altar; if a Bishop, he comes accompanied by two Deacons and sits on the Throne.

The Clerks recite the Psalm proper to the day: then read the Prophecies and the Apostolic Epistles, adding the Anthem according to the lesson.

The Epistle ended, the Deacon who is to read the Gospel, and another bearing incense, present themselves to the Celebrant, the one to receive the benediction, the other to have the incense blessed.

Then the Deacon says:

Orthi.

'Op∂oí, *a Greek word signifying:* stand up.

The Celebrant then turns to the people, blesses them with the Cross, and says:

Peace † be with all.

CLERKS. — And with thy spirit.

DEACON. — Listen with fear.

The Deacon who is to chant the Gospel:

The holy Gospel according to S^t. etc.

CLERKS. — Glory be to Thee, O Lord our God.

DEACON. — Proschume.

A Greek word signifying: be attentive.

42

CLERKS. — It is God who speaks.

The Gospel ended, all say :

Glory be to Thee, O Lord our God!

The Celebrant goes to the altar and they recite the Credo, which the Deacon says aloud :

We believe in one God, the Father Almighty, Maker of Heaven and Earth, and of all things visible and invisible; and in one Lord Jesus Christ, the only Son of God, born of the Father before all worlds. God of God, Light of Light, Very God of Very God, begotten, not made, consubstantial with the Father, by whom all things were made in Heaven and Earth, visible and invisible; who for us men and for our salvation, came down from Heaven, was incarnate by the Holy Ghost, of the Virgin Mary and **was made man, and who took from her, Body, Soul and Spirit, and all that in man is, in truth and not in fiction; who suffered, was crucified and buried; who rose again the third day, and ascended with the same body into Heaven, where he sat at the right hand of God, and whence He shall come with the same body in the glory of the Father, to judge the quick and the dead; whose reign shall have no end. We believe also in the Holy Ghost not created, but perfect, who proceedeth from the Father and the**

Son, who spake in the Law, the Prophets and the holy Gospel; who descended into the Jordan, who announced the Envoy (CRIST) and dwelt in the Saints. We believe in one Universal and Apostolic Church, in one baptism, in penance for the expiation and remission of sins, in the resurrection of the dead, in the Eternal judgment of body and soul, in the kingdom of Heaven, and in the life Eternal.

Those who say that there was a time when the Son existed not, and when the Holy Ghost existed not, or that they were created out of nothing; or that the Son of God and the Holy Spirit are of another essence; or that they are mutable; Those who thus say, the Catholic and Apostolic Church excommunicates.

DEACON. — Give thy benediction, Lord Priest.

The Priest adds the profession of St. Gregory, the Illuminator:

As for us, we glorify Him who was before all ages, adoring the Holy Trinity and the only Divinity of the Father, Son and the Holy Ghost, now, and throughout all ages.

The Deacon who has read the Gospel, offers it to the Celebrant, to kiss.

DEACON. — Let us pray God for peace.

CLERKS. — Lord have mercy upon us.

DEACON. — Let us pray with faith, and implore our Lord God and our Redeemer, Jesus Christ, at this hour of sacrifice and prayer, to make us acceptable; may He listen to the voice of our prayers, accept the requests of our hearts, efface our sins and have mercy on us. May our orisons and prayers be always accepted by His sovereign majesty, and may He grant us to confirm ourselves in the unity of the faith and in the justice of good works, that our Lord all-powerful may bestow upon us the grace of His mercy, pity and save us.

CLERKS. — Save us Lord.

DEACON. — Let us pray God that we may pass this hour of the Holy Mass, and the present day, in peace.

CLERKS. — Grant it us, Lord.

DEACON. — Let us pray God, that the Angel of peace may guard us.

CLERKS. — Grant it us, Lord.

DEACON. — Let us pray God for the propitiation and the pardon of our sins.

CLERKS. — Grant it us, Lord,

DEACON. — Let us pray God that the great and powerful virtue of the Holy Cross may help our souls.

CLERKS. — Grant it us, Lord.

DEACON. — Let us pray for the unity of the true and holy faith.

CLERKS. — Lord, have mercy upon us.

DEACON. — Let us commend ourselves, and one another mutually, to God.

CLERKS. — O Lord, we commend ourselves to Thee.

DEACON. — Have mercy upon us, O Lord our God, according to Thy great mercy; let us say with one accord.

CLERKS. — Have mercy upon os, O Lord.

(This invocation is thrice repeated).

During these alternate chaunts the Priest prays in a low voice, with extended arms:

Our Lord and Redeemer, Jesus Christ, who art

rich in mercy and generous in the gifts of Thy beneficence; Thou who hast at this hour suffered the torments of the Cross, and death, for our sins, and who hast abundantly showered the gifts of Thy Holy Spirit on the blessed Apostles, we pray Thee, O Lord, to make us participants of Thy divine gifts, of the forgiveness of sins, and of the reception of the Holy Ghost.

DEACON. — Give thy benediction, Lord Priest.

PRIEST ALOUD. — That we may be found worthy gratefully to glorify Thee, together with the Father and the Holy Ghost, now, and throughout all ages.

Peace † be to all.

CLERKS. — And with thy spirit.

DEACON. — Let us worship God.

CLERKS. — In thy presence, Lord Priest.

PRIEST ALOUD. — By Thy peace, O Christ Redeemer, which passeth all understanding, fortify us, and secure us from all evil; include us in the number of Thy true adorers, who worship Thee in spirit and in truth; for to the Holy Trinity belong glory, power and honour, now, etc.

Blessed be our Lord, Jesus Christ.

CLERKS. — Amen.

DEACON. — Give thy benediction, Lord Priest.

PRIEST. — May the Lord God bless † you all.

DEACON. — Let no Catechumen nor one whose faith is doubtful, nor one who is in the performance of penance, nor impure person, approach these divine mysteries.

CLERKS. — The Body of our Lord, and the Blood of our Redeemer are about to be here present. The heavenly Powers invisibly sing and proclaim with uninterrupted voice: Holy, Holy, Holy, Lord God of hosts!

DEACON. — Sing hymns to the Lord our God, spiritual hymns, O singers, in the sweetest tones.

Here the Clerks sing the Hagiology according to the mystery of thd day, whilst the Deacons carry to the altar the sacred bread and Chalice of benediction. — When they begin to sing they draw the great curtain: then the Bishop takes off the vestments of honour, such as the mitre and Pallium: if the Celebrant is not a Bishop, he only takes off his cap which he deposes on the altar. — Then they undraw the curtain.

48

An innumerable Choir of Angels and of the heavenly hosts descended from Heaven with the king, the only Son, singing and saying: This is the Son of God. Let us then all cry: Rejoice O ye Heavens! be overjoyed, foundations of the universe, for the ever-living God has appeared on Earth, and has conversed with men to save our souls.

For Maundy-Thursday.

Thou who sittest majestically enthroned in light, O ineffable Word of God, descending from the celestial heights for Thy creatures, Thou hast deigned this day to sit at table with Thy disciples. Seized with astonishment and amazement, the Seraphim and Cherubim stood around, and the principalities of the heavenly hosts shouted: Holy, Holy, Holy, Lord God of Hosts.

For Easter.

What god was ever like unto our God? He was crucified for us, buried, and is risen again. He has been acknowledged God by the world, and has gloriously ascended into Heaven. Come, O people, sing His praises with the Angels: Holy, Holy, Holy, Thou art, O Lord our God.

For Sundays, the Festivals of the Church, and of the Angels.

O God who hast filled Thy holy Church with
the Angelic hierarchy, myriads of Archangels are
present, and millions of Angels serve Thee. Yet from
men also Thou art pleased to receive benediction in
these mysterious words : Holy, Holy, Holy, Lord God
of Hosts.

For the Feasts of Martyrs.

O holiness of the saints, how great and terrible
Thou art! the Angelic hosts praise Thee saying :
Glory to God in the Highest, and peace on Earth.

For Fast days, and days on which the dead are prayed for.

Receive in memory of the departed, this Sacrifice, O Holy Father, full of love, and receive their
souls among Thy Saints in the kingdom of Heaven ;
for we offer Thee this Sacrifice with faith to obtain
the reconciliation of Thy Divinity, and the repose
of their souls.

For the Feasts of Prophets, Apostles and Pontiffs.

Thou art all-powerful, O Lord of Hosts, King
Eternal, who sittest above the highest heavens, who

illuminatest Thy creatures, and who, by a prodigy of
humility, art descended on earth. We offer Thee
this Sacrifice, and we exalt Thy holy name, O
Lord, who crownest Thy Saints (N. N.) : for they
are our intercessors in Thy kingdom, O Lord all-
powerful.

While the singers chaunt the hymns, two Deacons transport the offerings with the usual ceremony, and the Priest, inclined towards the
altar, recites, in a low voice, the following prayer.

None of us, soiled with passions and carnal desires, is worthy to approach Thine altar, or to serve
Thy royal glory, Thy service being great and terrible even for the heavenly hosts. But Thou O incomprehensible Word of the Father, by Thine immense
beneficence, hast made Thyself man, and our sovereign Priest, and, master of all, Thou hast confided
to us the Priesthood for this holy ministry and for
Thy unbloody Sacrifice ; for Thou art the Lord our
God who rulest all creatures in Heaven and Earth,
who art seated on the Cherubim as on a throne,
Lord of the Seraphim and King of Israel : who alone
art holy and dwellest in the Saints. I pray Thee,
Thou alone beneficent and prompt to grant our
prayers, throw a glance of pity on me a sinner and
Thy useless servant, and purify my soul and spiri
from all malignant stain ; and by virtue of Thy Hol
spirit make me, who am invested with priestly grac

worthy to assist at the holy altar, and to consecrate
Thine Immaculate Body and Thy precious Blood.
Humbly bending before Thee, I implore Thee not to
turn Thy face from me, and not to exclude me from
the number of Thy servants, but make me worthy
to offer Thee this oblation, sinner and unworthy servant as I am, since Thyself art Offering and Offered,
Receiver and Giver, O Christ our God! and to Thee
we give glory with the Father without beginning,
and the Holy and beneficent Spirit, now and
ever, etc.

The holy Offerings being taken to the altar, the Priest incenses
them, and washes his hands, saying the Psalm: Lavabo, etc.

DEACON. — Let us pray God for peace.

CLERKS. — Lord, have mercy upon us.

DEACON. — With faith and holiness, let us pray
before the holy altar of God, filled with profound
dread; with a pure conscience and void of offence,
without hypocrisy and duplicity; not with a spirit
wavering and doubtful in the faith, but with upright
actions sincere thoughts, submissive hearts and perfect faith: filled with charity and abounding in good
works, let us be earnest in prayer before the holy
altare of God, and we shall find grace in the day of
manifestation and in the second coming of our Lord

and Redeemer, Jesus Christ, who saves us and shows mercy to us.

CLERKS. — Save us, Lord, and have mercy upon us.

While the Deacon recites the preceding exhortation, the Priest, with extended arms, prays in a low voice.

O Lord God of Hosts, creator of all beings, Thou who hast called all things out of chaos into life, and who, honouring our earthly nature, hast lovingly raised it to the ministry of so awful and so inexplicable a Sacrament; Thou, Lord, to whom we offer this Sacrifice, accept from us this offering, and accomplish it in the Sacrament of the Body and Blood of Thine only Son. Grant this cup to be an expiatory remedy for the sins of him who drinks it.

DEACON. — Give thy benediction, Lord Priest.

PRIEST. — By the grace and mercy of our Lord and Redeemer, Jesus Christ, to whom, as to Thee, O Father, and to Thy Holy Spirit belong glory, power and honour, now etc.

Peace † be to all.

CLERKS. — Amen, and with thy spirit.

DEACON. — Let us adore God.

CLERKS. — In thy presence, Lord Priest.

DEACON. — Salute each other with a holy kiss; and ye who are not fit to partecipate in the divine mystery, retire to the door and pray.

The Deacon kisses the altar and the arms of the Celebrant, then he brings the salute to others.

THE CLERKS SING. — Christ showed Himself to us; God, the Supreme Being, has built His palace here. The voice announcing peace has sounded; salvation has been proclaimed, enmity has been destroyed, and charity has penetrated every where. Now, open your lips, O Ministers of God, bless with one accord, the consubstantial and inseparable divinity, to whom the Seraphim sing the hagiology.

At the more solemn Feasts they sing the following Passages.

DEACON. — You who with faith surround this sacred and royal altar, behold Christ the king seated there, surrounded by the Heavenly Hosts.

CLERKS. — With eyes turned towards Heaven, let us pray, saying: Remember not our sins, but pardon us in Thy clemency. We bless Thee with the Angels, and with the saints we say : Glory to Thee, O Lord.

Deacon. — Let us assist with fear, with respect, with modesty and with fixed attention.

Clerks. — Before Thee, O Lord.

Deacon. — Christ the Immaculate Lamb of God, offers Himself as victim.

Clerks. — Mercy and Peace and Sacrifice of benediction.

Deacon. — Give thy benediction, Lord Priest.

The Priest turns and gives the benediction with the crucifix which he holds, saying :

May the grace † and the love and the divine and sanctifying virtue of the Father, the Son, and the Holy Spirit be with you all.

Clerks. — And with thy spirit.

Deacon. — Hold the doors with circumspection

and precaution (*); lift up your hearts with fear unto the Lord.

. CLERKS. — We lift them up unto Thee, O Lord God Almighty.

DEACON. — Give thanks unto God with your whole heart.

CLERKS. — It is meet and right so to do.

Whilst the assistants alternately sing, the Priest says the following prayer in a low voice, with joined hands:

It is very meet and right to worship Thee without ceasing, and diligently to glorify Thee, O God the Father Almighty, Who by the operation of Thine Inscrutable and Co-Creating Word, hast removed the impediment of the Malediction ; Which (Word) having formed His people the Church, has appropriated to Himself those who believe in Thee, and, in the human nature assumed in the womb of the Blessed Virgin, has vouchsafed to dwell amongst us ; and, condescending to fulfil divinely a work entirely new, has restored heaven to

(*) There is here an allusion to an ancient custom which is no longer observed, that of requiring the Catechumens and all those who had not the privilege of assisting at the sacred Mysteries, to leave the Church.

earth. Wherefore, He in whose sight the glorious bands of Heaven's untiring watchers dare not stand, bowed down by the dazzling inaccessible light of the Deity, having made himself very man for our salvation, has vouchsafed to unite us in spiritual harmony with the celestial choirs.

Deacon. — Give thy benediction, Lord Priest.

Priest. — To sing with one voice, with the Seraphim and Cherubim the songs of hagiology, and to cry aloud and full of confidence with them :

Clerks. — Holy, Holy, Holy, Lord God of Hosts. Heaven and Earth are full of the Majesty of Thy glory : Blessing in the Highest. Blessed be Thou, who art come, and art to come in the name of the Lord ! Hosannah in the Highest.

On certain Feast-days, before the Sanctus, the Deacon sings the following hymn.

For our true and in all fulfilled redemption we give Thee thanks O Christ our Lord. At the miracle of Thy (Resurrection, Ascension, Birth) the Virtues sing praises, the Seraphim are filled with dread, the Cherubim tremble, and the Heavenly Powers and Principalities, ranged in joyous groups, cry with a loud voice and say, etc.

This hymn ended, all the Clergy kneel. The Priest, whilst the Clerks chaunt the Sanctus, says in a low voice, with outstretched arms.

Holy, Holy, Holy, Thou art verily, and the plenitude of holiness. Can words express Thine immense mercy, Thou who, from the earliest age hast taken care of sinful man and hast helped him in divers manners, by the Prophets, by the sanction of the Law, by the Priesthood, and by the oblation of heifers figurative of another sacrifice ? At the end of the established time, annulling the sentence of our debts, Thou hast given us Thine only Son, debt and debtor, sacrificed and consecrated, lamb and heavenly bread, sovereign Priest and Sacrifice ; for He is the distributor and He is constantly distributed among us without ever being consumed. Being made man in truth and not in appearance and being incarnate in the womb of the Virgin Mary, Mother of God, He traversed all the passions of human life, pure from sin, and of his own free will made his way to the Cross, the salvation of the world and our redemption.

Then taking the bread in his holy, divine, most immaculate and venerable hands, He blessed † it, gave thanks, brake it and gave it to his chosen and holy disciples seated at table with him, saying :

4*

DEACON. — Give thy benediction, Lord Priest.

Priest, aloud.

Take, eat,

This is my Body

which is given, for you and for many, for the expiation and remission of sins.

CLERKS. — Amen.

PRIEST, IN A LOW VOICE. — In like manner, having taken the cup, He blessed it †, gave thanks, drank, and gave it to his holy and chosen disciples seated at table with him, saying:

DEACON. — Give thy benediction, Lord Priest.

Priest, aloud.

Drink ye all of it,

This is my Blood, the Blood of the new Testament, which is shed for you and for many for the expiation and remission of sins.

CLERKS. — Amen.

O heavenly Father, who for us hast delivered up to death Thy Son bowed down under the weight of our sins, by His Blood shed for us, we implore Thee to have mercy on Thy flock.

During this time the Priest says in a low voice:

And to do this in remembrance of Him, such was the command of Thy beneficent and only Son, who, descending into the deepest abysses of death, in the flesh, and having victoriously thrown down the gates of hell, manifested Thee as the only true God, the God of the living and the dead.

The Priest takes the Offerings with both hands, makes the sign of the Cross with the Bread and the Cup, and says in a low voice:

We, then Lord, obeying this command, presenting Thee the salutary Sacrament of the Body and Blood of Thine only Son, call to mind His salutary sufferings for us, His crucifixion, source of life, His sepulture during three days, His happy resurrection, His triumphant ascension proper to a God, and the seat taken by Him at Thy right hand, O Father ; and we acknowledge and bless His second coming, terrible and glorious.

DEACON. — Give thy benediction, Lord Priest.

The Priest, having laid the Offerings on the altar, says aloud:

We offer Thee Thy gifts in all and for all.

CLERKS. — In all things be blessed, O Lord ; we bless Thee, we praise Thee, we give thanks unto Thee, we pray to Thee, O Lord our God.

Whilst this is being sung, the Priest prays low, with outstretched arms :

O Lord our God, we praise Thee justly, and we render Thee incessant thanks who without regard to our unworthiness, hast made us ministers of a Sacrament so tremendous and as ineffable; not by our own merit, of which we acknowledge ourselves void, but confiding solely in Thy boundless mercy, we dare approach the ministry of the Body and Blood of Thine only Son, Our Lord and Redeemer, Jesus Christ, to whom belong glory, power and honour, now, and throughout all ages.

DEACON. — Give thy benediction, Lord Priest.

PRIEST. — Peace † be to all.

CLERKS. — And with thy spirit.

DEACON. — Let us adore God.

CLERKS. — In thy presence, Lord Priest.

O Son of God, who hast offered Thyself to the Father as a sacrifice for our reconciliation, and hast given Thyself to us as the Bread of Life, we implore Thee, by the shedding of Thy Divine Blood to have pity on the flock redeemed by Thee at so high a price.

The Priest during this time, bending over the altar, says in a low voice:

We adore Thee, we pray and supplicate Thee, O beneficent God, to pour upon us, and upon the gifts which we offer Thee, Thy co-eternal and co-essential Holy Spirit;

He then makes the sign of the Cross upon the Host:

By whose means, Thou hast made the consecrated bread, to become verily, the Body of our Lord Jesus Christ; (*This is repeated three times*).

He then makes the sign of the Cross on the Chalice:

By whose means, Thou hast made the consecrated cup, to become verily the Blood of our Lord Jesus Christ; (*repeated thrice*).

He then makes the sign of the Cross on the two species :

By whose means, Thou hast made the consecrated bread and wine, to become verily the Body
and Blood of our Lord Jesus Christ, changing them
by Thy Holy Spirit. (*repeated thrice*).

At every benediction the Deacon answers in a low voice :

Amen.

DEACON. — Give thy benediction, Lord Priest.

PRIEST ALOUD. — To us all here united, may the
approach unto this Sacrament be not condemnation,
but expiation and pardon of our sins.

Then the Deacon incenses the people, who rise :

CLERKS. — O Spirit of God, who, descended
from Heaven, workest by our hands the Sacrament
of Jesus Christ of whose glory Thou partakest ; by
the shedding of His Blood we pray Thee to give repose to the souls of the departed.

*The Priest no longer extends his hands over the Offerings, but
drops them, and says low :*

Grant by the virtue of this Sacrifice, charity,
stability and peace throughout the universe, to Thy

holy Church, to all orthodox Bishops, to Priests and Deacons, to Kings, Princes and people, to travellers, navigators and prisoners; to those exposed to peril, to the weary, and to all those who are at war with barbarians.

By this Sacrifice, grant us healthy weather fertility to the country, and to all the sick a speedy cure.

By this Sacrifice, give repose to those who sleep in the peace of the Lord, Bishops, Priests, Deacons; to all the Clergy of Thy holy Church, to all laymen and women who have quitted this life in the faith.

DEACON. — Give thy benediction, Lord Priest.

PRIEST, ALOUD. — We pray Thee, to visit us, also, O beneficent God.

CLERKS. — Remember us, Lord, and have mercy upon us.

PRIEST. — We beg you in this Holy Sacrifice to commemorate the holy Virgin Mary, the Mother of God, S.ᵗ John the Baptist, S.ᵗ Stephen the first Martyr, and all the saints.

CLERKS. — Remember them, Lord, and have mercy upon us.

64

All the Deacons assemble on the side of the Gospel to chant the following prayer:

We beg you to make memorial of the holy Apostles, Prophets, Doctors, Martyrs and of all holy Pontiffs, apostolic Bishops, Priests, orthodox Deacons and all the Saints.

CLERKS. — Remember them, Lord, and have mercy upon us.

On Sundays:

DEACONS. — Let us adore the blessed, praised, glorified, admirable and divine Resurrection of Christ.

According to the Dominical Feasts, they vary the following words thus:

Let us adore the Holy Cross, *or* the Ascension, *or* the coming of the Holy Ghost, *or* the dominion of our Lord, etc.

CLERKS. — Glory to Thy Resurrection, O Lord.

For the Feasts of the Saints:

DEACON. — We beg you to make memorial in this Sacrifice of N. N. Prophet, *or* Apostle, *or* Martyr, *or* Pontiff, holy and dear to God, whose memory we have to-day celebrated.

CLERKS. — Remember him, Lord, and have mercy upon us.

DEACON. — We beg you to make memorial, in this holy Sacrifice, of our Prelates, and of our first holy illuminators : of Thaddaeus and Bartholomew Apostles, of Gregory the Illuminator, of Aristaces, of Vertanes, of Ussigh, of Gregory, of Niersès, of Issagh, of Daniel, of Khat, of Mesrob Doctor, of Gregory Naraghèse, of Niersès Glaèse, and of all the Pastors and Archpastors of Armenia.

CLERKS. — Remember them, Lord, and have mercy upon us.

DEACON. — We beg you to make memorial, in this holy Sacrifice, of those holy solitaries and virtuous monks inspired by God, Paul, Anthony, Pol, Macaire, Onuphre, Marc abbot, Serapion, Nil, Arsène, Evagre, of the Johns, the Simons, the holy Oschians, of the Succhianites, and of all the holy Fathers and their disciples throughout the universe.

CLERKS. — Remember them, Lord, and have mercy upon us.

DEACON. — We beg you to make memorial, in this holy Sacrifice, of the faithful and holy Kings Abgare, Constantine, Tiridate and Theodosius, of all pious and holy Kings, and of Princes having the fear of God.

CLERKS. — Remember them, Lord, and have mercy upon us.

All the Deacons assemble before the altar, and sing:

We beg of you to make mention, in this holy Sacrifice, of all the faithful in general, men and women, old men and children of all ages, who repose with faith in Christ.

CLERKS. — Remember them, Lord, and have mercy upon us.

During this commemoration, the Priest says in a low voice:

Remember, Lord, and have mercy, and bless Thy holy Catholic and Apostolic Church, which Thou hast redeemed by the precious blood of Thine only Son, and delivered by the virtue of the holy Cross: grant her a solid and continual peace.

Remember, Lord, and have mercy, and bless all orthodox Bishops who, in the true doctrine, preach among us the word of truth.

All the Deacons assemble on the side of the Epistle.

DEACON. — Give thy benediction, Lord Priest.

PRIEST, ALOUD. — Above all, preserve to us in the right doctrine, our holy Pope N. N., and our venerable Patriarch N. N. *or* Archbishop *or* Bishop.

They thus make commemoration of Catholic Prelates only.

Then the Deacon passing on the left side of the altar chants the following ascription of praise, but in the form of prayer, which no one shall dare to change as if it were made without reason, for by it Bishop Chosroe the Great explained the custom of the ancients.

We render Thee thanks and praise, O Lord our God, for this holy and immortal Sacrifice, offered on this holy altar, imploring Thee to grant that it may turn to the sanctification of our lives. In favour of this Sacrifice, grant charity, firmness and the much desired gift of peace to the whole universe, to the holy Church, to all orthodox Bishops; and especially to our holy Pope N. N., to our venerable Patriarch, *or* Archbishop, *or* Bishop, and to the Priest who is offering this Sacrifice. We pray for the maintenance and victory of Christian Kings, and religious princes: we pray and implore Thee for the souls of the departed, particularly those of our Prelates, and of the founders of this holy Church, and for the souls of all those who sleep in its shadow. We pray Thee for the deliverance of our brethren become slaves, for mercy towards the people here present, for repose for those who, in faith and holiness have finished their mortal career in Christ. We beg you to make memorial of all those in this Holy Sacrifice.

CLERKS. — In all, and for all.

In unison with this chant of the Deacon, the Priest says low, the following prayer :

Remember, Lord, and have mercy, and bless Thy people here assembled, both the offerers, and the givers of the offerings for the celebration of this holy Sacrifice, and be favorable to them in all things useful and necessary.

Remember, Lord, and have mercy, and bless the pious men who offer their gifts to Thy holy Church, those who compassionate the poor; and render them, in the measure of Thine innate liberality, a recompense hundredfold, in this life, and in the world to come.

Remember, Lord, and have mercy, and be favorable to the souls of the departed, and give them repose and light, and place them among Thy saints in the kingdom of Heaven, by rendering them worthy of Thy mercy.

Remember, Lord, the soul of Thy servant N. N., and have mercy upon him according to Thy great mercy, graciously grant him to enjoy the light of

Thy countenance, and (*if he lives*) save him from all peril of body and soul.

Remember, also, O Lord, all those who, living or dead, have recommended themselves to our prayers; direct their desires and ours to the best and most profitable end, granting us all imperishable felicity. Purify our thoughts, and make us temples worthy to receive the Body and Blood of Thine only Son, our Lord and Redeemer, Jesus Christ, to whom as to Thee, Almighty Father, and to the Spirit of life and sanctity, our liberator, belong glory, power and honour, now etc.

DEACON. — Give thy benediction, Lord Priest.

Priest, aloud, making the sign of the Cross on the people:

May the mercy of God and of our Redeemer, Jesus Christ, be † with you all.

CLERKS. — And with thy spirit.

DEACON. — Let us pray God for peace.

CLERKS. — Lord, have mercy upon us.

DEACON. — Let us pray God, with all the Saints we have commemorated.

CLERKS. — Lord, have mercy upon us.

DEACON. — Let us pray God by means of this holy and divine Sacrifice, offered on this holy altar.

CLERKS. — Lord, have mercy upon us.

DEACON. — Let us pray the Lord our God, who has accepted it in His holy, celestial and immaterial offertory, that He may deign to send us, in exchange, the grace and the gifts of the Holy Spirit.

CLERKS. — Lord, have mercy upon us.

DEACON. — Receive, save, have mercy, and keep us, Lord, by Thy grace.

CLERKS. — Save us, Lord, and have mercy upon us.

DEACON. — Let us pray God, making memorial of the holy Virgin Mary, Mother of God and of all the Saints.

CLERKS. — Lord, have mercy upon us.

DEACON. — Let us again pray for the unity of our true and holy faith.

CLERKS. — Lord, have mercy upon us.

DEACON. — Let us commend ourselves, and each other mutually to the Lord God all-powerful.

CLERKS. — We commend ourselves to Thee, O Lord.

DEACON. — Have mercy upon us, O Lord, according to Thy great mercy; let us say all together:

CLERKS. — Lord, have mercy upon us; (*repeated thrice*).

During this time the Priest says in a low voice:

God of truth and Father of mercy, we thank Thee for this favour by which Thou hast honoured our sinful race beyond the blessed Patriarchs. By them Thou wert called God, by us it pleaseth Thee to be affectionately named Father. We pray Thee, O Lord, that this new name so honourable for us, may shine every day more in Thy holy Church.

DEACON. — Give thy benediction, Lord Priest.

PRIEST, ALOUD. — Allow us with filial voice to invoke Thee as our Heavenly Father, saying:

CLERKS. — Our Father, who art in Heaven! hallowed be Thy name, Thy kingdom come, Thy will be done on Earth as it is in Heaven. Give us this day our daily bread, and forgive us our trespasses, as we forgive them that trespass against us; abandon us not to temptation, but deliver us from evil. Amen.

While the Clerks chant the Pater, the Deacon incenses the people who stand, and the Priest says in a low voice:

Lord of Lords, God of Gods, King eternal, Creator of all creatures, Father of our Lord, Jesus Christ, let us not fall into temptation, but deliver us from evil, and save us from snares.

DEACON. — Give thy benediction, Lord Priest.

PRIEST, ALOUD. — For Thine is the kingdom, the power and the glory, for ever and ever. Amen.

Peace † be to all.

CLERKS. — And with thy spirit.

DEACON. — Let us adore God.

CLERKS. — In thy presence, Lord Priest.

They kneel, and all profoundly inclined, the Priest says in a low voice :

O Holy Spirit! Thou who art the source of life and of mercy, have pity on this people who, kneeling, adores Thy Divinity, keep them pure and without stain : penetrate their souls with the disposition figured by the present posture of the body, that they may partake of the inheritance of Thy future gifts.

DEACON. — Give thy benediction, Lord Priest.

PRIEST, ALOUD. — Through Jesus Christ our Lord, to whom, as to Thee, O Holy Spirit, and to the Almighty Father, belong glory, power and honour, now and throughout all ages.

DEACON. — Proschume, (*be attentive*).

The Priest taking the Holy Host, and raising it, says :

To the Holiness of the Saints.

CLERKS. — Alone Holy, only Lord, Jesus Christ, in the Glory of God the Father, so be it.

DEACON. — Give thy benediction, Lord Priest.

PRIEST. — Blessed be the Holy Father, very God.

CLERKS. — So be it.

DEACON. — Give thy benediction, Lord Priest.

PRIEST. — Blessed be the Holy Son, very God.

CLERKS. — So be it.

DEACON. — Give thy benediction, Lord Priest.

PRIEST. — Blessed be the Holy Ghost, very God.

CLERKS. — So be it.

DEACON. — Give thy benediction, Lord Priest.

Then the Priest, raising the cup, says :

Blessing and glory be to the Father, to the Son, and to the Holy Ghost, now and throughout all ages.

CLERKS. — So be it. Holy Father, Holy Son, Holy Spirit: blessing to the Father, to the Son, and to the Holy Ghost, now etc.

While the Clerks sing, the Priest prays in a low voice:

Look upon us, O Lord Jesus Christ, from Heaven Thy Sanctuary, and from the glory of Thy kingdom, come to sanctify and save us. Thou who, seated near Thy Father, art here sacrificed, deign to give us Thine Immaculate Body and Thy precious Blood, and to all this people, by our hands.

Then he adores and kisses the altar, and taking the Holy Body, dips it entirely in the pure Blood, saying with a low voice:

O Lord our God, who, from the name of Thine only Son, hast called us Christians, and hast given us regenerating baptism for the remission of sins, and hast rendered us worthy to receive the sacred Body and Blood of Thine only Son, we pray Thee, O Lord, to render us worthy to receive this holy Sacrament in remission of sins, and to give Thee glory with grateful hearts, as well as to the Son, and to the Holy Ghost, now, and throughout all ages.

DEACON. — Give thy benediction, Lord Priest.

The Priest, turning towards the people, elevates the Holy Sacrament, making the sign of the Cross, and says aloud:

Let us partake holily of the holy, holy and precious Body and Blood of our Lord and Redeemer Jesus Christ, who, descended from Heaven, is distributed among us. He is life †, the hope of the resurrection, the expiation and pardon of sins. Sing to the Lord our God, sing to our immortal king, seated on the throne borne by the Cherubim.

DEACON. — Sing, O Clerks, to the Lord our God, in the sweetest tones, sing spiritual songs; for to Him are due psalms and benedictions, allelujahs and spiritual songs. Sing psalms O Ministers, and bless the Lord of Heaven.

They draw the little curtain, and the Priest holding the Sacred Host, kissing it, says:

What blessing and what thanks can we render for this Bread and this Cup? We bless Thee, alone, O Jesus, with Thy Father and the Holy Spirit, now, and throughout all ages.

He adds:

I confess, and I believe that Thou art the Christ, The Son of God, who hast borne the sins of the world.

Dividing over the Chalice the Sacred Host into three parts, he puts one into the Chalice, saying:

Plenitude of the Holy Spirit.

Holding the other parts, he prays *in a low voice*, whilst the Clerks sing :

CLERKS. — Christ sacrificed is distributed among us. Allelujah !

He gives us His Body as food, and He sheds forth His Holy Blood upon us. Allelujah !

Approach the Lord and fill yourselves with His light. Allelujah !

Taste and see how gracious the Lord is. Allelujah !

Bless the Lord in the Heavens. Allelujah !

Bless Him in the high places. Allelujah !

Bless Him all ye his Angels. Allelujah !

Bless Him all ye his Powers. Allelujah !

Sometimes, after these benedictions the Clerks add a canticle appropriate to the feast of the day :

Monday.

O true light and splendour of the Father, Emanation and image of His essence, Word and generation, who hast erected the holy Church on seven hills ; ready victim led to sacrifice, permit us to nourish ourselves at the table of Thy wisdom; have mercy upon us.

Tuesday.

Bread of life and of immortality, holy and ineffable food, awe inspiring Sacrament, who art descended from Heaven to vivify man, ardent and vivifying Life, give to us an hungred the food of thy tenderness. Have mercy upon us.

Wednesday.

Gate of Heaven and road to Paradise, Lord of Heaven, blessed by the celestial choirs; who hast distributed Thy pure Body and Blood to the Apostles, purify us, that we may participate in Thy holy Sacrament. Have mercy upon us.

Thursday.

Word of the Father, and holy Pontiff, praised by the Angels in the highest Heavens; Thou who, sacrificed on the Cross in Thy flesh, hast shed Thy Blood for the salvation of the world; blot out our sins by the virtue of Thy vivifying and expiatory Blood, which giveth salvation and life. Have mercy upon us.

Friday.

Spiritual and corner stone, our sovereign Master, Jesus Christ, glorified by the Angels; who, on the Cross, hast caused to gush out, from Thy sacred side, a source abounding in immortality, which has watered the entire universe; permit us, athirst, to drink from Thy Cup of salvation. Have mercy upon us.

Saturday.

Lamb of God, always sacrificed and always living, glorified by the immortal hosts, who, pure from all fault, wast led to death and sacrificed to reconcile us with the Father, efface the sins of the world, and remember the souls of our departed, who died firm in the faith. Have mercy upon us.

While the Clerks chant, the Priest, holding the two fragments of the Host over the Chalice, says in a low voice:

O holy Father, who hast called us by the same name as Thine only Son, and hast enlightened us by regenerating baptism; make us worthy to receive this holy Sacrament in remission of our sins, imprint in us the grace of Thy Holy Spirit, as in Thine Apostles, who, in nourishing themselves with it, have become the purifiers of the universe. Now, O beneficent Father, grant that this communion may have on me the effect of the communion of the disciples, dissipating the darkness of my sins; behold not my unworthiness, and withdraw not the grace of Thy Holy Spirit; but, according to Thine immense love, grant that this Sacrament may be an expiation for our sins, and absolution of our trespasses, as our Lord Jesus Christ has said and promised it: He who eateth of my Body and drinketh of my Blood, shall live eternally. Grant, then, that this may purify us from all stain, that those who eat and drink, may

give blessing and glory to Thee, O Father, with the
Son, and the Holy Spirit, now, etc.

Peace † be to all.

I thank Thee, O Christ, our King that, all des-
titute of merit as I am, Thou hast rendered me worthy to participate in Thy Holy Body and Blood. I
pray Thee, O Lord, that it may not serve to condemnation, but to the expiation and pardon of my
sins, to the salvation of soul and body, and to the
accomplishment of all good works. May this divine
mystery sanctify my breath, my spirit and my body,
that I may become the temple and habitation of the
Holy Trinity, and be found worthy, in union with
Thy saints, to glorify Thee, with the Father and the
Holy Spirit, now, and throughout all ages.

Prayer of St. Chrysostom.

I give Thee thanks, I exalt Thee, I glorify Thee,
O Lord my God, Thou hast rendered me worthy on
this day to partake of Thy Divine and fearful Sacrament, of Thine Immaculate Body and Thy precious
Blood. Now taking for intercessors these holy and
sacred objects, I implore Thee to preserve me during this day, and every hour of my life in Thy holiness, that ever remembering Thy clemency, I may
live with Thee, who, for the love of us hast suffered,
wast dead, and art risen again. O Lord God, Thou
who hast sealed my soul with Thy precious blood,

let not the infernal destroyer approach me. Thou who art all-powerful, purify me by the virtue of this divine mystery, from all deadly works; Thou, who alone art without sin. Strengthen my life against every temptation, that the enemy may retire, full of shame and confusion at every attack. Direct my thoughts, my words and ways. Dwell ever within me, according to Thine infallible promise: He who eats my Body and drinks my Blood, dwells in me, and I in him. Thou hast said it, O all-merciful; grant that the effect may correspond to this divine and irrevocable decree, for Thou art a God of mercy, of clemency and of love, the giver of all good; and to Thee belong glory, together with the Father, and Thy Holy Spirit, now, and throughout all ages.

Then signing himself with the sign of the Cross, the Priest asks of God divers favours for himself, for the people, for every body, even for those who have offended him, and for his enemies, and full of reverential fear, he partakes of the Sacred Body and drinks of the Cup saying:

May Thine incorruptible 'Body be to me †, the source of life; and may Thy Holy Blood be the propitiation and remission of my sins!

Then they open the little curtain, the Deacon receives the Holy Sacrament, then the Deacon takes the Chalice and turning towards the people, says aloud:

Approach ye with fear and faith, and communicate holily.

Clerks, aloud. — Our God and our Lord, has appeared to us. Blessed be He who cometh in the name of the Lord.

They give the holy communion to those who are prepared, then the Priest makes the sign of the Cross on the People, saying aloud:

Lord, save † Thy people, and bless Thine inheritance, conduct them, exalt them, now and to the end of all ages.

Then they draw the great curtain, and the Bishop puts on, anew, the robes of honour, which he had taken off at the moment of the offertory:

Clerks. — We are loaded, O Lord, with Thy benefits, nourished as we are with Thy Body and Blood. Glory be to Thee in the highest Heavens, to Thee, who hast satisfied us. Thou, who nourishest us without ceasing, bestow on us Thy spiritual blessing. Glory be to Thee in the highest Heavens, to Thee, who hast satisfied us.

During this interval, the Priest says in a low voice:

We thank Thee, Almighty Father, who hast prepared for us this sure port, the holy Church, temple of sanctity, where is glorified the most Holy Trinity. Allelujah!

We thank Thee, O Christ our king, who hast given us life through Thy vivifying body and Thy precious blood. Forgive us, and be merciful to us. Allelujah!

We thank Thee, Spirit of truth, who hast renewed the holy Church; preserve us pure in the faith of the most Holy Trinity, till the consummation of ages. Allelujah!

DEACON. — Let us pray God for peace, with still more fervour, after having received with faith the divine, celestial, immortal, immaculate and most pure Sacrament: Let us thank God.

CLERKS. — We thank Thee, O Lord, who hast nourished us at Thine immortal table, by giving us Thy Body and Blood for the salvation of the world, and for the life of our souls.

PRIEST, IN A LOW VOICE. — We thank Thee, O Christ our God, who hast given us such food of goodness, that we may live holily. Through it preserve us pure and immaculate, dwelling in us by Thy divine protection: direct us in the way of Thy holy and beneficent will, by which, strengthened against every will of Satan, we may listen to Thy voice and follow Thee alone, Almighty and true Pastor, and may obtain the place prepared in Thy heavenly kingdom, O our God, Lord, and Redeemer, Jesus Christ, who art blessed with the Father and the Holy Spirit, now, and throughout all ages.

Peace † be to all.

To Thee inscrutable, incomprehensible, three-fold creating Essence, beneficent Holy Trinity, inseparable and consubstantial, belong glory, power and honour, now, and throughout all ages.

When the Celebrant has finished this prayer, the Deacon says:

Give thy benediction, Lord Priest.

Then they open the great curtain, and the Celebrant holding the Gospel, turns, with the Deacons, towards the people, and says aloud:

Thou Lord, who blessest those who bless Thee, and who sanctifiest those who hope in Thee, save Thy people and bless Thine inheritance; preserve the plenitude of Thy Church; purify those who have piously visited the majesty of Thy house. Glorify us by Thy divine virtue, and forsake not those who hope in Thee. Give peace to the whole world, to the Churches, to the Priests, to christian Kings and their armies, and to all this people; for every good gift and every thing perfect descends from on high, from Thee who art the Father of light, and to Thee belong glory, power and honour, now, and throughout all ages.

The Clerks say thrice:

Blessed be the name of the Lord, now, and to the consummation of ages.

PRIEST. — Accomplishment of the Law and the

Prophets, Christ our God and Redeemer, who hast fulfilled all the prescriptions ordained by the Father, fill us with Thy Holy Spirit.

DEACON. — Orthi. (*Let us rise*).

PRIEST. — Peace † be to all.

CLERKS. — And with thy spirit.

DEACON. — Listen with fear.

PRIEST. — The holy Gospel according to S^t. John.

CLERKS. — Glory to Thee, O Lord our God.

DEACON. — Proschume, (*be attentive*).

CLERKS. — It is God who speaks.

PRIEST. — In the beginning was the Word. (*to verse the* 18*th*).

During Easter, they chant the Gospel of S. John XXI, 15 : So when they had dined. (*to verse* 20).

The Gospel ended, the Clerks answer :

Glory to Thee, O Lord our God.

DEACON. — By the holy Cross let us pray God, that by it He may deliver us from sin, and save us by His merciful grace. O Lord our God all powerful, save us and have mercy upon us.

THE PRIEST SAYS THREE TIMES. — Lord have mercy upon us.

Keep us in peace, O Christ our God, in the shadow of Thy holy and venerable Cross; deliver us from the enemy, visible and invisible; make us worthy to thank and to glorify Thee with the Father and the Holy Spirit, now, etc.

CLERKS. — I will bless the Lord always; may His blessing be ever on my lips.

The Priest making the sign of the Cross on the people, says :

Be blessed † by the grace of the Holy Spirit; go in peace, and may the Lord be with you all! Amen.

Then inclining to the altar he says:

Lord God Jesus Christ, have mercy upon me.

Then he goes to the Sacristy, where he takes off the sacred vestments.

Whilst they recite the psalms, a Priest distributes the blessed bread to the people.

HYMN.

O Church, mother of the faith, asylum of holy marriage!
   Splendid nuptial chamber!
   Dwelling of the immortal Spouse,
   Who has adorned Thee with eternal ornaments.

Thou art another admirable Heaven,
   Elevated from glory to glory,
   Who regeneratest us by means of holy Baptism,
   And makest us sons shining as the light.

Who distributest to us this purifying bread,
   And givest us to drink this awe-inspiring blood;
   Who raisest us to the highest degree
   Even to share the destiny of the celestial Intelli-
                       [gences.

Come then, O Sons of the new Sion,
   Approach the Lord with purity,
   Taste and see how our Lord
   Is good and powerful.

The Ark of the Covenant was a type representing Thee;
    But Thou art the type of the Supreme Tabernacle.
    It has broken the adamantine gates, (*)
    Thou hast torn from their foundation the gates of
                                      [hell.

It triumphed over the Jordan,
    Thou, over the sea of universal wickedness.
    Its leader was Joshua,
    Thine is Jesus, the only Son of the Eternal Father.

This bread is the Body of Jesus Christ,
    This cup is the Blood of the new Testament;
    The greatest of mysteries is revealed to us,
    God manifests Himself to us.

Here is Christ Himself, the Divine Word,
    Who sitteth at the right hand of the Father,
    Who, sacrificed here amongst us,
    Effaceth the sins of the world.

He is blessed in all Eternity
    With the Father and the Holy Spirit,
    Now, for ever and ever,
    Throughout all ages.

(*) The gates of Jericho.